Drawing Support 2:
Murals of War and Peace

Bill Rolston

First published 1995
by
Beyond the Pale Pubications
PO Box 337
Belfast BT9 7BT
Tel: +44 (0)1232 645930

British Library Cataloguing-in-Publication Data
A catalogue record for this book is available from the British Library.

ISBN 0 9514229 7 9

Printed by
Colour Books Ltd
105 Baldoyle Industrial Estate
Baldoyle
Dublin 13

Acknowledgements

Thanks to Anna Eggert and Mike Tomlinson for support and
encouragement.

For Anna

She keeps my feet on the ground

Contents

The Story so Far

The tradition of mural painting in the North of Ireland is almost a century old. Beginning around 1908, loyalist artisans — coach painters, house painters, etc. — began to paint large outdoor murals each July. The timing was no accident; the murals were part of the annual celebrations of the Battle of the Boyne, one of a series of battles for the English throne between King James II and his son-in-law, Prince William of Orange. The battle took place on July 1, but with subsequent changes in the calendar, was celebrated in later years on July 12, known as "the Twelfth". The annual celebrations involved marches, flags, banners, bunting — and murals.

The victory of King William III (King Billy, as he is known) ushered in a period of consolidated British rule in Ireland, which included the "Protestant ascendancy". A key element in this ascendancy was the existence of "penal laws" whose purpose was the containment of the Catholic and Presbyterian populations of Ireland. The later incorporation of Presbyterians through the Act of Union of 1800 (which established the United Kingdom of Britain and Ireland) left the Catholics of Ireland at the bottom of the social hierarchy.

The annual celebration on the Twelfth was redolent with all these historical memories of victory and defeat. The significance of the celebration increased with the establishment of the Northern Ireland state following partition in 1920. The ritual became not merely a reaffirmation of unionist identity, but of a new variant in the Protestant ascendancy, a state ruled by one party and founded on the exclusion of a large minority of the population, the nationalists. Where the state's first prime minister could boast of having "a Protestant parliament and a Protestant state", marching, flying flags and painting murals took on extra significance. They became in effect a civic duty, recognised and legitimised as such by the state and its governing party.

Given their exclusion, nationalists did not paint murals. Their culture was marginalised, relegated to the private spaces of Catholic church halls, Gaelic sports fields, and private clubs. Nationalist opposition to partition took a number of forms, most obviously the sporadic military campaign of the Irish Republican Army (IRA). But the streets and public places were unionist. Republicans had less freedom to march and fly flags; they did not paint murals.

That situation changed with the hunger strike of 1981. Republican prisoners protested at the loss of "special category status", and eventually ten of them died. Nationalists and republicans took to the streets in support of the prisoners; huge marches took place and young nationalists began "drawing support" for the hunger strikers on the walls. The republican mural tradition was born.

With the end of the hunger strike, republican mural artists found other themes — the electoral strategy of Sinn Féin (the republican party), international comparisons, media censorship, etc. The new-found confidence of republicanism was symbolised in many ways, not least the manner in which they now claimed public space through marches and mural painting. The range of themes and styles evident in the murals is a striking illustration of this confidence.

By the 1980s unionism was less confident than it had been. Although militant loyalists engaged in a military campaign against nationalists and republicans, it was clear that the old unionist certainties were under siege. Again, the murals provided a window into the changed mentality. King Billy murals became less frequent, and in their stead were depictions of flags and other inanimate symbols. From the mid-1980s on, unionist and loyalist opposition to the Anglo-Irish Agreement left its mark on the walls, with the proliferation of stark military images.

The Story Continues: Loyalist Murals

Drawing Support: Murals in the North of Ireland charted and documented this story up to the summer of 1992. Mural painters on both sides continued to paint murals on the same themes after that date.

Given the centrality of King Billy, it appears paradoxical that his image was so uncommon in loyalist murals in the 1990s. Although new images of King Billy crossing the Boyne appeared from time to time (see plates 1-3), there were fewer such images overall. Moreover, some were in advanced stages of decay, pointing to the failure of some communities to maintain the tradition of re-touching the paintings prior to each Twelfth. It would be possible to exaggerate the significance of this decline. All the same, it does appear to be highly symbolic of a crisis in loyalist identity.

The crisis is starkly revealed in the Fountain area of Derry, the last Protestant working class enclave on the city side of the River Foyle. Here existed the oldest extant King Billy, painted and repainted for 70 years by three generations of the Jackson family. In the 1970s, when the area was being redeveloped, the Northern Ireland Housing Executive paid for the removal and reassembly of the wall and its mural. In 1994, the wall collapsed. Shortly before it did, a very different "King Billy" appeared briefly nearby (see plate 4). It portrayed a loyalist killer as King Billy. Michael Stone had attacked a republican funeral in Belfast in March 1988 with grenades and a handgun. He killed three mourners who had pursued him, before being rescued by the police. His action gained him hero status with many loyalists, including, one presumes, those who painted the Derry mural. But in 1990, Bobby Jackson, then 63 years old, articulated his disdain for such paramilitary murals and the young loyalists who painted them.

> "I don't like them at all because they're very political and it seems as if there's death about the town and destruction more than anything else. There's nothing beautiful about them. It's always something political. They can't think about their own town; they've lost out on history. It's a very sad thing."[1]

In this view, history is counterposed to politics and culture excludes militarism.[2]

Often the symbols that now graced the walls where King Billy used to have undisputed prominence were of inanimate objects. It was often possible to see where the mural painter (and indeed the group to which he owed allegiance) stood on the spectrum between British identity and Ulster identity. The Union Jack, the flag of the Union, could stand on its own (see plate 5), revealing a traditional British identity; alternatively, there might be no Union flag at all, depicting a more hard-line, Ulster independence attitude (see plate 6). But more often than not, the flag murals stated that the Union of England, Scotland (as represented by the blue and white flag of St. Andrew) and Northern Ireland was worth fighting for (see plate 7). Alongside the flags were emblems, insignia, etc; in one mural the coat of arms of the City of Derry appeared, showing a skeleton representing the experience of the Siege of Derry in 1689 (see plate 8).

The Red Hand of Ulster also figured prominently, whether traditionally represented (see plate 9), or clenched in a fist, a symbol of the UFF, Ulster Freedom Fighters (see plate 10), or encircled in barbed wire, the preferred depiction of the LPA, Loyalist Prisoners' Association (see plate 11). The Red Hand could also appear with other heraldic devices (see plate 12).

The most noteworthy fact about these murals depicting inanimate symbols was the stark absence of human beings. It was as if loyalist mural painters no longer knew where loyalist people fitted.

Moreover, the flags, shields, etc. seemed sure, indisputable, immovable. Yet the very robustness of this representation again disguises an underlying identity problem. These murals protest their confidence too much. As James Hawthorne, then Controller of BBC Northern Ireland put it:

> "The more the majority — or at least the highly loyal section of it — waves the Union flag and talks of loyalty, the more it strives to cover up its identity problem."[3]

Much less ambivalent were the murals which display members of loyalist military organisations, primarily the UFF (Ulster Freedom Fighters), the UVF (Ulster Volunteer Force), and the RHC (Red Hand Commando). Prior to the Anglo-Irish Agreement of November 1985 there were relatively few such murals, but each summer afterwards they appeared regularly. This change accurately reflects the rearmament of loyalist groups in the late 1980s as a result of a large shipment of guns from South Africa, arranged by a British agent within loyalism, Brian Nelson. By the early 1990s loyalists were killing more people than republicans were, and military imagery was the most common theme in loyalist murals. Balaclavas and automatic weapons abounded, whether the military *men* were shown in action (see plates 13-18) or posing with their weapons (see plates 19-22). Sometimes the weapons could stand alone as mute testimony to loyalist military action (see plate 23). These military murals did not obviously reveal the purpose of loyalist military action, nor against whom the weapons were directed. There was no hint that during "the troubles" overall loyalists killed more civilians than republicans did, or that by the 1990s they were killing more people each year than republicans were, despite official assertions of republicanism as the main problem.[4] But, to the nationalist or republican potentially at the receiving end of loyalist bullets, these murals were often sinister or threatening. And every now and again, the threat was spelt out. One mural in effect espoused 'ethnic cleansing'; "There is no such thing as a nationalist area of Northern Ireland, only areas temporarily occupied by nationalists" (see plate 24).

Among the military murals were also memorials to fellow members who "died in action" (see plates 25-27); less common were murals alluding to the comrades who were still alive, but imprisoned (see plates 28, 29).

Historical events and references were highlighted from time to time, but, unlike in the 1980s, there were no new murals depicting the Siege of Derry (1689) or the Battle of the Somme (1916). Instead, there were references to the original UVF (1912) and the B-Specials, a paramilitary loyalist police force of the unionist state between 1921 and 1969 (see plate 30). One such mural was part of a much larger complex of inter-related murals on the Newtownards Road in East Belfast. It depicts a B-Special and a member of the UDR, Ulster Defence Regiment, the successor to the B-Specials and later merged with the Royal Irish Rangers, another British army regiment — "Ulster's past defenders" (see plate 31). The mural to the right of this contains the statement: "Our message to the Irish is simple: hands off Ulster. Irish out. The Ulster conflict is about nationality". On the right of this is what has been to date the most astonishing image in a loyalist mural; behind a member of the East Belfast Brigade of the UDA (Ulster Defence Association), "Ulster's present day defenders", is "Cuchulainn, ancient defender of Ulster from Irish attacks over 2000 years ago" (see plate 32).

The apparent incongruity of the Cuchulainn image is striking. It is an exact reproduction of the bronze statue sculpted in 1911 by Oliver Sheppard, which later came to stand as the symbol par excellence of the nationalist Rising at Easter 1916. Cuchulainn's stand against the invading army of Queen Mebh of Connacht was seen by nationalists as representing the desperate gesture of the republican and socialist revolutionaries who declared a republic in the face of overwhelming odds. The statue came to occupy pride of place in the General Post Office in Dublin, which had been the headquarters of the insurgents.

Why then should such a symbol ever end up on a loyalist wall in East Belfast? The answer is in the attempt to create a history for unionists at least as ancient as that traditionally claimed by nationalists.[5] This attempt rested on the centrality of the Cruithin, or Picts, the pre-Celtic inhabitants of the north-east of Ireland and the south-west of Scotland. The Cruithin's power waned as the Celts, who had arrived in Ireland from continental Europe, expanded from the south and west of Ireland. Queen Mebh's attack on Ulster and Cuchulainn's defence were thus easily reinterpreted. Mebh was a Celt, Cuchulainn a Cruithin. Cuchulainn thus came to be seen as in effect the first UDA man, defending Ulster against the marauders from 'the south'.

The revisionist history has never been widely accepted in unionist circles, particularly among the more respectable and middle class Ulster Unionist Party, UUP. As a political symbol, Cuchulainn the loyalist seems to more easily represent the secessionist proposal of an "independent Ulster" espoused from time to time by the UDA, rather than the desire to integrate fully with Britain, a policy dear to the UUP.

Finally, there is a category of loyalist murals which are humorous in content. Such murals derive their iconography less from loyalism or Protestantism than from cartoons and popular culture; thus in Ballymena a loyalist Bart Simpson proudly stands on the neck of a rat with the head of Gerry Adams, President of Sinn Féin (see plate 33). Usually painted by young men associated with loyalist marching bands, one such mural alluded to the fact that the band concerned was barred from marching because of its drunken behaviour on a previous occasion (see plate 34).

Republican Murals in the 1990s

Despite its origins in a prison hunger strike, an event which could have been depicted solely in humanitarian terms, the republican mural tradition had from the start refused to distance itself from the reason the prisoners had ended up in prison. Murals portraying the "armed struggle" were common from 1981 on, but were less so in the 1990s. Central to these murals were the actions and personnel of the IRA (see plate 35). IRA men were depicted posing with their weapons or in action (see plates 36, 37). Often the weapons themselves came to stand for the military activity, whether the "barrack busters" of South Armagh, improvised from metal propane gas containers (see plate 38) or more conventional weapons. In one case, the words of the republican slogan "Tiocfaidh ár lá" (our day will come) were arranged in the form of an armalite (see plate 39). Memorials to fallen comrades also came into this genre (see plate 40).

The prison issue did not reach any similar crisis at any point after the conclusion of the 1981 hunger strike. Despite the mass prison breakout in 1983 and the festering issue of segregation between loyalist and republican prisoners in the 1980s and early 1990s, to all intents and purposes the hunger strike achieved most of the republican demands. That said, the continuation of "armed struggle" meant there was a constant supply of new recruits to the prisons to join those republicans already there on long and indeterminate sentences. In that situation, there were occasional reminders in the murals that people should not forget the prisoners as well as references back to previous prison issues, such as the 1981 hunger strike (see plate 41) and the case of Tom Williams (see plate 42). Williams had been executed in 1942 and his body buried in Crumlin Road prison, Belfast. By the 1990s there was a campaign for the release of his body from the prison yard for reburial in a republican grave.

Although the political aspirations and ideology of republicanism were spelt out in murals, for the most part this was not the case in the "armed struggle" murals. It was left to another set of murals on the general theme of repression and resistance to articulate republican aspirations and demands. Opposition to the presence and activities of the British

Army, including its Northern Ireland regiment, the UDR, was paramount (see plates 43, 44). Blatant acts of repression, such as the shooting dead of 14 civilians by the Paratroop Regiment during a peaceful civil rights march in Derry in 1972 (see plate 45), were addressed. In a more contemporary reference, as overwhelming evidence mounted in the 1990s of collusion between elements of the British forces and loyalist assassination squads, the issue was raised on walls (see plates 46, 47). A notorious case of collusion was that of Brian Nelson, a senior intelligence officer in the UDA who was also an operative for British intelligence for ten years. As well as successfully setting up a number of republicans for assassination, he was instrumental in arranging the shipment of weapons supplied clandestinely by the South African forces for use by loyalists (see plate 48).

Overall, as numerous murals declared, the ultimate aim of republicanism was "Brits Out" and "free Ireland" (see plates 49-52). The demands could be referred to directly, or obliquely, as in the reference to Cuchulainn, alluding not only to the Easter Rising of 1916 but also to the continuing willingness of republicans to take on overwhelming odds in the struggle for independence (see plate 53). From then to now, the murals inferred, the struggle continued in various ways, including the successful attempt, after many years of failure, of republican marchers from West Belfast to march to the centre of their city (see plate 54).

Republicans also involved themselves with some measure of success in elections. Murals urging people to "Vote Sinn Féin" were often humorous and drew on many sources (see plates 55-57), including the most unlikely one of the paintings of Norwegian artist Edvard Munch (see plate 58).

Finally, the existence of anti-imperialist and democratic struggles elsewhere was a source of inspiration to republican muralists. Where in the 1980s there had been references to South Africa, and Palestine, in the 1990s it was Euskadi and Mexico (see plates 59, 60). Nicaragua figured in a mural in the centre of Derry (see plate 61). It involved the collaboration of three muralists from Managua, Nicaragua, and three from Derry (Doire in Gaelic). More generally, another Derry mural took the words of South American guerrilla priest Camilo Torres as the central message in a powerful and controversial image (see plate 62).

25 Years On: The Peace Process

In August 1969 the residents of the Bogside in Derry had successfully kept the RUC and B-Specials at bay during three days of riots; this became known as the Battle of the Bogside. At the same time, loyalist mobs had burned out hundreds of nationalist residents in the Lower Falls area of Belfast. In response to these clear signs that the unionist government had lost control, the British government sent troops onto the streets of Derry and Belfast.

Twenty five years later these events were commemorated in a series of republican murals. Derry muralists of course recalled the Battle of the Bogside (see plates 63, 64), while in Belfast a mural celebrated "25 years of resistance", with images of women banging bin lids and soldiers with gas masks, modelled on photographs of events in the area in August 1969 (see plate 65).

But there was more than mere nostalgia involved in the timing of these murals. For some years previously Sinn Féin President Gerry Adams and the leader of the Social and Democratic Labour Party, John Hume, had been meeting to thrash out a common nationalist agenda for peace. Their announcement in the summer of 1993 that they had drawn up proposals which could guarantee a solution to the conflict became the catalyst for a sustained peace process. The British government was initially reluctant to participate in a process which they did not control, despite the earlier claims of their Secretary of State that Britain had no strategic interest in remaining in Northern Ireland. By the end of 1993, the production of a joint proposal, the Downing Street

Declaration, by John Major, the British Prime Minister, and Albert Reynolds, Taoiseach of the Irish Republic, seemed to snatch the initiative from Hume and Adams. The acceptance of both governments that there could be no united Ireland without the consent of unionists seemed to underwrite the political status quo; as one Belfast mural concluded at the time, "Nationalists sold out once again" (see plate 66).

But it soon became clear that the peace process would not be thwarted easily by the British. By the summer of 1994 it was clear that the political situation had changed. The republicans had made a gamble which, if it worked, could lead eventually to them engaging in negotiations for British withdrawal and a political settlement.

In this context the commemorative murals could be said to be looking back in order to look forward. These murals argued that twenty five years was enough. It was time for something different, time for peace, time for the British to go. "Time to go" became the key slogan of republican murals in the summer and autumn of 1994 (see plates 67, 68).

The most common image used in these murals was that of a poster painted by Irish artist Robert Ballagh (see plate 69). But there were variations on the theme, whether the reproduction of another famous photograph from early in "the troubles", showing two elderly women remonstrating with British paratroopers (see plate 70), or of a "Cormac" cartoon from *An Phoblacht/Republican News* (the republican newspaper), showing doves flying from Ireland to England, each with a British soldier in its claws. "Time for peace", says each dove; "time to go", replies each soldier (see cover plate).

Perhaps unsurprisingly, there was little sense of changing times in the contemporaneous loyalist murals — no commemoration of events a quarter of a century before, no references to a peace process. In Agnes Street, one slogan on a wall hijacked the republican slogan for loyalist purposes: "25 years. Time to go. Irish out of Britain. Eire, bring your dole scroungers back home".

Ceasefire

In retrospect, there seems to have been an almost effortless transition from the peace process of 1993/4 to the IRA ceasefire. However, that is not how it appeared to many at the time. Some believed that after 25 years the IRA were "wedded to violence" for its own sake and could never give it up. Even more sympathetic commentators could not easily foresee the IRA taking the ultimate gamble of, in effect, cashing in all its chips at once. But that is what happened when, on August 31 1994, the IRA announced a "complete cessation" of military action as of midnight.

The British were unwilling to concede a moral victory to their opponents, and began a protracted phase of finding fault and erecting obstacles. The IRA were disbelieved, their claims of ceasefire dismissed as cynical and opportunist. A "period of quarantine" would be necessary before the British government could engage in public exploratory talks with republicans. And the British took grave exception to the IRA's announcement of a "complete" cessation of military action, demanding instead commitment to a "permanent" cessation. From the IRA's point of view, this would have been tantamount to unconditional surrender.

For their part, republicans were anxious not merely to respond to the filibustering of the British, but also to articulate their own demands and aspirations in the changed political climate. Even though the ultimate goal was still the achievement of a united Ireland, more immediate demands were to the fore — the departure of the British army, the disbandment of the RUC, and the release of republican prisoners. All of these found expression on the walls of republican areas.

The first ceasefire mural in Belfast, painted one day after the IRA announcement, specified "the foundation stones for lasting peace" (see plate 71), while in South Armagh, the "sniper at work" signs now noted that the war was "on hold" (see plate 72).

A number of murals questioned the British commitment to the peace process (see plate 73), while others responded to British government objections by turning their words against them (see plate 74).

The argument that, for the British army, it was "time to go" continued to be made (see plate 75), but as the more general demand "demilitarise now" revealed, the indigenous forces, particularly the RUC, were also seen as a problem. Consequently, as troops were slowly withdrawn to barracks during daytime and as small numbers of them began to leave for Britain, the question of the RUC came to the fore (see plates 76-80). The means employed to get across the message of opposition to the RUC were often ingenious. "For Sale" signs were painted on RUC barracks (see plate 81), and one of a series of posters erected by the Community Relations Council, a quango, was doctored. Tapping into a popular sectarian myth that Protestants and Catholics can be distinguished by the distance between their eyes, the poster showed a close up of a face with the distance between the eyes measured out. The accompanying slogan was: "If you catch yourself thinking like a bigot, catch yourself on". Republicans on the Falls Road altered this, adding after the word "bigot", "join the RUC" (see plate 82).

The release of political prisoners was also a key element in the republican agenda following the ceasefire, and figured in many murals. Although the demand was for the release of all "POWs" (prisoners of war; see plates 83-87), frequently local areas listed the names of their own political prisoners in the mural (see plates 88, 89).

Five weeks after the republican announcement, loyalists also declared a ceasefire. Like republicans, loyalists demanded to be included in negotiations with the British. Similarly, the release of political prisoners was seen to be central to progress. But, beyond that, it was difficult to ascertain the exact nature of loyalist aspirations. Certainly, the departure of the British army and the disbandment of the RUC were not demands. And, given traditional divisions among loyalists regarding fuller integration within the United Kingdom on the one hand and independence from Britain on the other, there was no clear "national" or constitutional aspiration apparent in post-ceasefire statements from loyalists. At base, the different paramilitary groups, now ably represented by political parties (the UDA by the Ulster Democratic Party, and the UVF by the Progressive Unionist Party), demanded the right to remain loyalist. As loyalism has most often been represented as armed reaction (to IRA campaigns, British reforms, etc.), the paradox was that in many ways the ceasefire required loyalists to protest even more loudly than usual that there was definitely "no surrender".

The difficulty of representing a ceasefire without showing signs of capitulation was a particularly profound one for loyalist muralists. The original solution was to acknowledge simply that the capitulation was one-sided, that it was the IRA which had surrendered (see plates 90, 91), while at the same time stressing that the paramilitary potential of the loyalist groups was in no way diminished (see plates 92, 93).

By the summer following the ceasefire, 1995, it became clear that little had changed in the world of loyalist murals. Banners, posters and some murals demanded the release of political prisoners (see 94), but the more common imagery in murals was of armed men (see plates 95, 96). The images became, if anything, even more sinister than previously. In one mural a loyalist batters down a door while his colleagues wait with weapons at the ready to storm into the house (see plate 97). The identity of the victim behind the door, or why s/he was presumed to deserve the imminent fate, were not spelt out. "Prepared for peace, ready for war", stated another mural (see plate 98), but all of its symbolism pertained solely to war.

Murals: the Future

The lack of development in loyalist murals is disappointing. But the rather obvious point must be stressed that murals do not exist in isolation from the culture and politics of the society which spawns them. Given that, the difficulties faced by loyalist muralists are a specific variant on those faced by the wider loyalist and unionist community in a period of political transformation. Loyalism, with its central claim to maintain the past (see plate 99), does not switch easily to articulating the future; nor do its muralists easily find the themes and images of a future vision in the absence of that articulation.

In many ways it is easier for republicans, struggling to change political arrangements rather than simply to maintain the past. Although harking back to the past and its heroes (see plate 100), republicans have, as self-professed socialists and anti-imperialists, channels into a world-wide rhetoric of political opposition and political change. Given both these factors, the range of themes and images available to republican mural painters is relatively wide. Consequently, they have been able to turn their attention from time to time to other themes — nationalist culture in general (see plates 101-103), Gaelic games (104), unemployment (see plate 105), and AIDS and gay pride (as in two murals in Derry). During the summer after the republican ceasefire, a series of murals was painted in West Belfast under the auspices of Féile an Phobail, the West Belfast Community Festival, on the theme of the Great Famine of 1845-49 (see plates 106-110).

There have been no such developments on the loyalist side. Given their long tradition of mural painting, loyalists clearly have the skills, but not the political space, to allow them to paint on a wider range of themes. In attempting to develop that space, they do not need to feel compromised by the possible accusation of copying the imagery of republicans. There are countless examples from elsewhere they can follow.

Mural painting is a global phenomenon. There is folk art, as in Tanzania (where popular tales are depicted on the outside walls of cafes), and religious art, as in Egypt (where a person who has visited Mecca can paint images of Islam on the outside walls of their house). Anti-imperialist murals are common, as in Nicaragua under the FSLN in the 1980s. And even in developed societies such as Germany and England there are murals on unemployment, racism, feminism and a range of other themes.

But the prime contender for the accolade of "mural heaven" has to be California, with over 1,000 murals in Los Angeles and around 600 in the San Francisco Bay area. There are countless murals on themes such as ethnic pride and opposition to racism. Unemployment, drugs, gang rivalry and warfare, landlord exploitation, and solidarity with people in struggle elsewhere, such as the Palestinians (see plate 111), are common. Women are to the forefront in painting on themes of central importance to their gender (see plate 112).

The seeds of some of this are already there in republican murals. Hopefully the republican mural tradition, despite its origins in war, is now well enough established to survive the ceasefire and progress to painting visions for the future of a society building a just peace. As for the possibilities that the much older loyalist tradition of mural painting can develop likewise, we can only keep our fingers crossed.

Footnotes:

1. Bobby Jackson, interviewed in BBC Radio Ulster's "Across the Line", November 11, 1990.
2. In 1994 a replica of this mural was painted on a wall designated to the memory of Bobby Jackson; see plate 99.
3. James Hawthorne, speech to Edinburgh International Radio Festival, 21 August 1981.
4. See Malcolm Sutton, *Bear in Mind These Dead: An Index of Deaths from the Conflict in Ireland, 1969-1994*, Belfast, Beyond the Pale Publications, 1994
5. See Ian Adamson, *The Cruithin*, Belfast, Pretani Press, 1974

Plate 1
Blythe Street, Belfast, 1990.
King Billy crossing the
Boyne. Painted for
tricentenary of Battle
of the Boyne.

Plate 2
Bond's Street, Derry, 1991.
King Billy crossing
the Boyne.

Plate 3
Larne, County
Antrim, 1993.
King Billy crossing
the Boyne.

Plate 4
Fountain area, Derry, 1993.
Michael Stone,
depicted as King Billy
crossing the Boyne.
Stone was in prison after
having killed three
mourners at a republican
funeral in Belfast
in 1988.

Plate 5
Percy Street, Belfast, 1992.
Union Jack, and
emblems of
Ulster Volunteer Force and
Protestant Action Force.
"We will never accept a
united Ireland.
Ulster still says no."

Plate 6
Newtownards Road,
Belfast, 1993.
Flags, Red Hand of Ulster
and slogan of
Ulster Young Militants,
youth wing of
Ulster Defence Association
- "Terrae filius"
(son of the earth).
"Ulster's Freedom Corner."

Plate 7
Roden Street,
Belfast, 1994.
Union Jack, flag of
St. Andrew (Scotland)
and Ulster shield.
Emblems of
Ulster Freedom Fighters
and Roden Street
Defence. Two armed
Ulster Defence
Association members
and emblem of Ulster
Defence Association:
"Quis separabit"
(Who will separate).

Plate 8
Bond's Street, Derry, 1991.
Union Jacks and coat of
arms and motto of
Londonderry:
"Vita veritas victoria"
(Life truth victory).

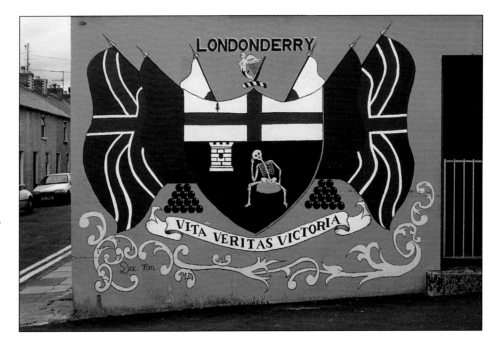

Plate 9
Portavogie,
County Down, 1994.
Union Jack, Ulster flag
and Red Hand of Ulster.

Plate 10
East Way, Rathcoole,
Newtownabbey,
near Belfast, 1993.
Red Hand of Ulster as
clenched fist. Slogan of
Ulster Young Militants,
youth wing of
Ulster Defence Association:
"Terrae filius"
(son of the earth).

Plate 11
Crimea Street,
Belfast, 1995.
Red Hands of Ulster:
as clenched fist,
symbol of the
Ulster Freedom Fighters,
and entwined in
barbed wire,
symbol of
Loyalist Prisoners'
Association.
Also emblem of Ulster
Defence Association.

Plate 12
Templemore Avenue,
Belfast, 1995.
Heraldic symbols
in honour of East Belfast
Protestant Boys Flute Band.
Painted in memory of
J. Boyd and
R. Cowan.

Plate 13
Highfield Drive,
Belfast, 1993.
Armed loyalists of
Ist Battalion,
A Company of
Ulster Freedom Fighters,
founded 1973, along with
Ulster flag, flag of
St. Andrew (Scotland)
and clenched
Red Hand of Ulster.

Plate 14
Doagh Road,
Newtownabbey,
near Belfast, 1992.
Armed loyalists of
Ulster Freedom Fighters,
founded 1973.

Plate 15
Dee Street, Belfast, 1993.
Armed loyalist of
Ulster Volunteer Force, with
emblem of Ulster Volunteer Force:
"For God and Ulster".

Plate 16
Snugville Street, Belfast, 1994.
Armed loyalists of
2nd Battalion, C Company of
Ulster Freedom Fighters.
"Ulster Freedom Fighters will resist
any Eire involvement in our country."

Plate 17
Roden Street,
Belfast, 1994.
Armed loyalist of
A Battalion,
Ulster Freedom Fighters.
"It is not for glory we
fight, nor riches, nor
honours – but for
freedom alone. Which no
good man loses but
with his life."

Plate 18
Snugville Street,
Belfast, 1994.
Armed loyalist with
Ulster Defence Association
emblem.
"UFF rocket team
on tour, West Belfast, 94."

Plate 19
King's Road,
Belfast, 1993.
Armed loyalist of
5th Battalion,
Ulster Defence Association,
Tullycarnet, with
emblems of
Ulster Defence Association,
Ulster Young Militants,
Ulster Freedom Fighters
and Loyalist
Prisoners' Association.

Plate 20
Carrington Street,
Belfast, 1994.
Armed loyalists of
Ulster Volunteer Force,
with flags and emblem of
Ulster Volunteer Force.

Plate 21
Newtownards Road,
Belfast, 1994.
Armed loyalist of
Ulster Freedom Fighters,
East Belfast.
"For as long as
one hundred of us remain
alive we shall never in
any way consent to
submit to the
rule of the Irish ..."

Plate 22
Hazelfield Street,
Belfast, 1993.
Armed loyalists of
2nd Battalion,
West Belfast Brigade of
Ulster Freedom Fighters,
with emblem of Ulster
Freedom Fighters.

Plate 23
Stroud Street,
Belfast, 1994.
Weapon of
Ulster Freedom Fighters.

Plate 24
Percy Street,
Belfast, 1994.
"There is no such thing
as a nationalist area of
Ulster, only areas
temporarily occupied by
nationalists."
"In remembrance of all
those who have given
their lives and their
freedom in the struggle
to keep
Ulster Protestant."

Plate 25
Sandy Row,
Belfast, 1994.
Memorial to dead
members of the
Ulster Defence Association,
in particular
Brig. J. McMichael,
and emblem of Ulster
Defence Association.

Plate 26
Roden Street,
Belfast, 1993.
Memorial to
Brig. J. McMichael of
Ulster Defence Association,
and emblems of Ulster
Defence Association,
Ulster Defence Force and
Loyalist Prisoners'
Association.

Plate 27
Disraeli Street,
Belfast, 1994.
Memorial to Lt. Col. Trevor King
of B Company, 1st Belfast Battalion of
Ulster Volunteer Force,
with emblem of
Protestant Action Force.

Plate 28
Percy Street,
Belfast, 1993.
Union Jacks, Ulster shield,
and emblems of
Ulster Volunteer Force,
Ulster Defence Association,
Protestant Action Force,
and
Young Citizen Volunteers.
"Shankill supports all the
loyalist prisoners."

Plate 29
Symons Street,
Belfast, 1992.
In support of
loyalist prisoners.

Plate 30
Derrycoole Way, Rathcoole,
Newtownabbey,
near Belfast, 1994.
In memory of
Ulster Volunteer Force of
1912, with emblem of
Ulster Volunteer Force and
flags of Ulster
Volunteer Force and
Young Citizen Volunteers.

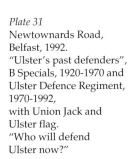

Plate 31
Newtownards Road,
Belfast, 1992.
"Ulster's past defenders",
B Specials, 1920-1970 and
Ulster Defence Regiment,
1970-1992,
with Union Jack and
Ulster flag.
"Who will defend
Ulster now?"

Plate 32
Newtownards Road, Belfast, 1992.
"Ulster's present day defenders",
East Belfast Brigade of Ulster Defence Association,
with Cuchulainn,
"ancient defender of Ulster from Irish attacks over 200 years ago".

Plate 33
Ballymena, 1991.
Bart Simpson as
loyalist, standing on
neck of Gerry Adams,
portrayed as a rat.
"Garryduff Road
loyalists."

Plate 34
Roden Street,
Belfast, 1992.
Roden Street Defenders
Flute Band.

Plate 35
Near Creggan, South Armagh,
photograph taken 1994.
IRA, Irish Republican Army.

Plate 36
Hillside Terrace, Newry,
County Down, 1994.
Armed republican. "Sniper at work."

Plate 37
Carnagat Road, Newry,
County Down, 1994.
Armed republican,
"Óglaígh na hÉireann"
(Volunteers of Ireland,
Irish Republican Army),
with sunburst, symbol of
Na Fianna Éireann,
youth wing of
Irish Republican Army.

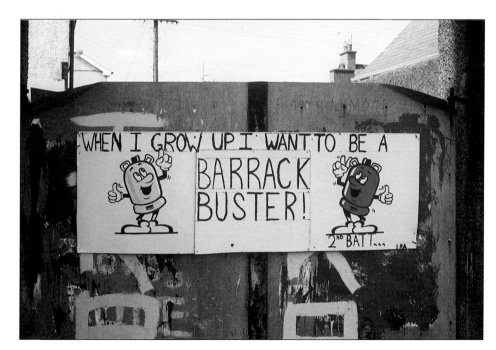

Plate 38
Crossmaglen, South
Armagh, 1993.
"When I grow up I want
to be a barrack buster."
2nd Battalion,
Irish Republican Army.

Plate 39
Off Springhill Park,
Strabane,
County Tyrone,
photograph taken 1993.
"Tiocfaidh ár lá"
(Our day will come)
in form of
Armalite rifle.

Plate 40
New Lodge Road,
Belfast, 1993.
Memorial to dead
members of
Irish Republican Army,
with Celtic cross,
armed republican,
Cuchulainn, Easter lily,
and sunburst.

Plate 41
Rossville Street,
Derry, 1991.
Portraits of Patsy O'Hara
and Mickey Devine,
Irish National
Liberation Army hunger
strikers from 1981,
and call to
"Celebration of
Resistance"
in Belfast.

Plate 42
Kashmir Road,
Belfast, 1995.
In memory of
Tom Williams,
executed in 1942.

Plate 43
Barcroft Park, Newry,
County Down,
photograph taken 1994.
Women with bin lids,
protesting
at British army
snatch squad.

Plate 44
Barcroft Park, Newry,
County Down,
photograph taken 1994.
British army snatch
squad in action.

23

Plate 45
Fahan Street,
Derry, 1992.
Portraits of 14 victims
of British Army
paratroop regiment,
Bloody Sunday,
1972.

Plate 46
Beechmount Avenue,
Belfast, 1990.
Union Jack and
head and skull
of loyalist assassin.

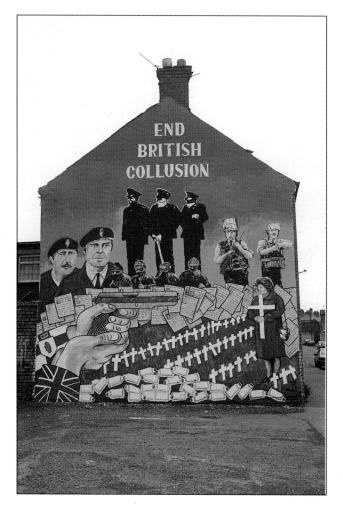

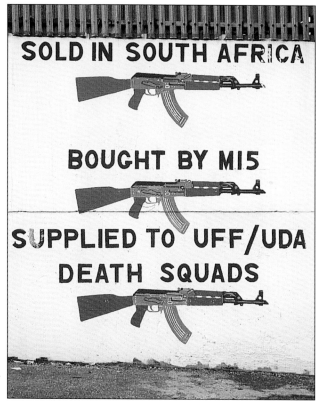

Plate 47
Oakman Street, Belfast, 1994.
"End British collusion", with members
of loyalist paramilitary groups,
Ulster Defence Regiment and
Royal Ulster Constabulary.

Plate 48
Springhill Avenue, Belfast, 1994.
Loyalist weapons,
"sold in South Africa, bought by
MI5, supplied to
UFF/UDA death squads".

Plate 49
High Street, Derry, 1993.
"Brits out, keep Éire tidy."

Plate 50
Beechmount Avenue, Belfast, 1990.
"Free Ireland", with manacled hand,
Easter lily, shields of four provinces of Ireland,
and burning General Post Office,
Caisc (Easter) 1916.

Plate 51
Ballycolman Road,
Strabane,
County Tyrone,
photograph taken 1993.
"Troops out now", and
emblem of British
Troops Out Movement.

Plate 52
Springhill Avenue,
Belfast, 1992.
Armed republicans.
"800 years of resistance."

Plate 53
Armagh, 1991.
Cuchulainn, four
provinces of Ireland, and
"Mise Éire,
mór mo gloir"
(I am Ireland,
great is my glory).

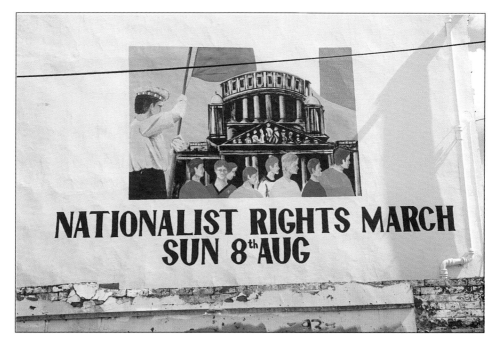

Plate 54
Dunville Street,
Belfast, 1994.
Marching republicans on
"nationalist rights march"
at City Hall, Belfast.

Plate 55
Waterford Street,
Belfast, 1992.
Sinn Féin election mural,
with plaque to
Nora McCabe, killed by
plastic bullet, 1981.

Plate 56
Lecky Road,
Derry, 1993.
Sinn Féin election mural.
"Shout with one voice."

Plate 57
Rossville Street,
Derry, 1992.
Sinn Féin election mural.
"Vote with your feet."

Plate 58
Rossville Street,
Derry, 1993.
Sinn Féin election mural.
"Give them that
screamin' feeling!"

Plate 59
Rosnareen Avenue,
Belfast, 1992.
Mural in solidarity
between Euskadi
and Ireland.
"Dhá chine aon croimhlint"
(Two peoples, one struggle).

Plate 60
Ballymurphy Road,
Belfast, 1992.
Ireland-Mexico solidarity
mural, with member of
Óglaigh na hÉireann
(Irish Republican Army),
James Connolly
(Irish revolutionary),
Emiliano Zapata
(Mexican revolutionary)
and United Farm Workers
member.
"You can kill the
revolutionary but not
the revolution."

Plate 61
Butcher Street,
Derry, 1992.
Doíre (Derry)-Managua
mural.

Plate 62
Rossville Street,
Derry, 1991.
Central America
Week mural.
"The Christian who is
not a revolutionary
is living
in mortal sin."

Plate 63
Rossville Street,
Derry, 1994.
Boy with gas mask and petrol bomb
during Battle of Bogside, 1969.

Plate 64
Strabane Old Road,
Gobnascale,
Derry, 1994.
Youth throwing petrol
bomb during
Battle of Bogside, 1969.

Plate 65
Dunville Street,
Belfast, 1994.
Burnt-out house,
British soldiers
and women
with bin lids during
early days of
"the troubles".

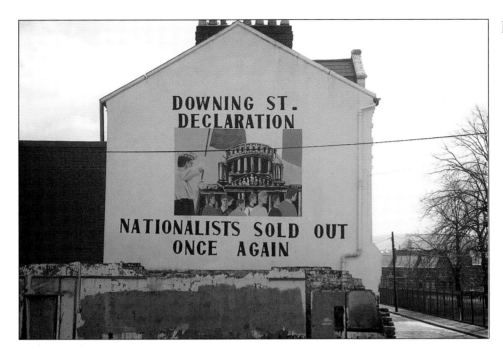

Plate 66
Dunville Street,
Belfast 1994.
Republicans marching.
"Downing Street
Declaration.
Nationalists sold out
once again."

Plate 67
Killeen,
County Armagh, 1994.
British soldiers leaving
by helicopter.
"Slán abhaile"
(safe home).
"Time for peace,
time to go."

Plate 68
Whiterock Road,
Belfast, 1994.
British soldier on patrol,
with republican demands.
"Slán abhaile"
(safe home).
"Fag ár sraideanna"
(leave our streets).

Plate 69
Ardoyne Avenue,
Belfast, 1994.
British soldiers leaving.
"Slán abhaile"
(safe home).
"25 years, time to go."

Plate 70
Donegall Road,
Belfast, 1994.
Local women and
British paratrooper.
"The spirit of freedom."

Plate 71
Falls Road,
Belfast, 1994.
Building blocks showing
republican demands and
aspirations.
"The foundation stones
for lasting peace."

Plate 72
Near Creggan,
South Armagh, 1995.
Armed republican.
"Sniper at work - on hold."

Plate 73
New Lodge Road,
Belfast, 1995.
Lark hampered by
Union Jack ball and chain,
with shields of
four provinces of Ireland.
"Who really
wants peace?"

Plate 74
Beechmount Avenue,
Belfast, 1994.
Response to John Major,
republican demands for
"a just and lasting peace".

Plate 75
Rossville Street,
Derry, 1995.
Time to go for
British soldiers,
police,
judges and
capitalists.

Plate 76
New Lodge Road,
Belfast, 1995.
Royal Ulster Constabulary
member with
plastic bullet gun.
"Remember the victims of
plastic bullets."

Plate 77
Racecourse Road,
Shantallow,
Derry, 1995.
Royal Ulster Constabulary
member,
victim of plastic bullet,
and lark in barbed wire.
"Peace means an end to
all killing.
Demilitarise now."

Plate 78
Jasmine Way, Twinbrook,
near Belfast, 1995.
RUC in action.
"Disband the RUC."

Plate 79
Whiterock Road,
Belfast, 1995.
Royal Ulster Constabulary
member with
plastic bullet gun.

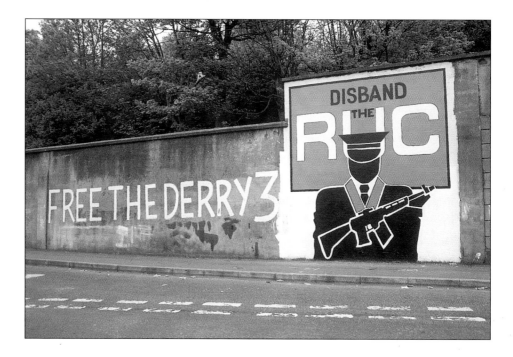

Plate 80
Lecky Road,
Derry, 1995.
Armed Royal Ulster
Constabulary member
wearing sash of the
Orange Order.
 "Disband the RUC."

Plate 81
Andersonstown
Police Barracks,
Glen Road, Belfast, 1994.
"For sale."
"Slán" (goodbye).

Plate 82
Waterford Street,
Belfast, 1994.
Amended
Community Relations
Council poster.
"If you catch yourself
thinking like a bigot,
join the RUC."

Plate 83
Westland Street, Derry, 1994.
Dove/fist breaking chain,
with names of POWs (prisoners of war) from Derry.
"700 Irish political hostages. Release them now."

Plate 84
Crossmaglen,
South Armagh, 1995.
"Saoirse anois"
(freedom now) for
prisoners of war.
"You stood by us then,
remember us now."

Plate 85
Crossmaglen,
South Armagh, 1995.
Prisoners,
male and female.
"Saoirse" (freedom).
"Release republican
prisoners now."

Plate 86
Creggan,
South Armagh, 1995.
Prisoner behind bars,
with shields of
four provinces of Ireland.
"Release all
political prisoners."

Plate 87
Donegall Road,
Belfast, 1995.
Dove carrying keys,
green ribbon and
"Saoirse" (freedom).

Plate 88
Almond Close,
Twinbrook,
near Belfast, 1994.
Candle in barbed wire
and names of local
prisoners.
"Saoirse" (freedom).

SID WALSH.
MICHAEL TIMMONS.
SEAN McMAHON.
KEVIN McLOUGHLIN.
EUGENE GILMARTIN.
DAVID McKAY.
RUARI McCARTNEY.
LOUIS IRVINE.

BRENDAN FLYNN.
DANNY CALDWELL.
SEAN FERRY.
FÉILIM Ó hADHMAILL.
PATRICK MURRAY.
JIMO REILLY.
PHILLIP MANNING.
GERRY HANRATTY.
GERARD LOUGHRIN.

94 Saoirse 94

Plate 89
Lenadoon Avenue,
Belfast, 1995.
Names of prisoners
from local area.
"Tiocfaidh ár lá."

free our POWs

Tíocfaidh ar Lá·

RORY DOUGAN
STEPHEN CANNING
DEE SULLIVAN
JOHN TRAINOR
MICHAEL BENNETT
MICHAEL DUFFY
JOHN SHANNON
JIMMY MARTIN
THOMAS FOX
LIAM McNALLY
DANNY CALDWELL

NOEL HEALY
SID WALSH
BOW WEIR
ROSENA BROWN
KEVIN CARDWELL
BRENDAN FERRAN
CIARAN FERRY
LIAM McCOTTER
PAT McCOTTER
NED FLYNN

Plate 90
Shankill Road,
Belfast, 1994.
Ulster Volunteer Force
 slogan.
"On behalf of the
loyalist people of the
Shankill Road
we accept the
unconditional surrender
of the IRA."

Plate 91
Dover Place,
Belfast, 1994.
Ulster Freedom Fighters,
2nd Battalion, slogan.
"I.R.A. Ran Away in 69.
I.R.A. Surrendered in 94."

Plate 92
Woodstock Link,
Belfast, 1994.
Armed loyalists and emblem of
Ulster Volunteer Force.
"Ulster Volunteer Force
1912-1994.
Still undefeated."

Plate 93
Blythe Street,
Belfast, 1994.
Emblem of
Ulster Defence Association.
"For as long as
one hundred of us
remain alive
we will never, never
(in any way) consent to
the rule of the Irish..."

Plate 94
Shankill Road,
Belfast, 1995.
Prison camp and Red
Hands breaking
chain. "For peace.
All gave some.
Some gave all.
Free the prisoners."

Plate 95
Shankill Road,
Belfast, 1995.
Armed loyalists and
memorial to members of
the Ulster Volunteer Force.
"Lest we forget."

Plate 96
Shankill Road,
Belfast, 1995.
Armed loyalists of
2nd Battalion, C Company,
Ulster Freedom Fighters,
with clenched
Red Hand of Ulster.
"Simply the best."

Plate 97
Dover Place, Belfast, 1995.
Armed loyalists of 1st Battalion, West Belfast,
of Ulster Volunteer Force, breaking down door,
with emblems of Ulster Volunteer Force, Protestant Action
Force and Young Citizen Volunteers.
"Compromise or conflict."

Plate 98
Mount Vernon Road, Belfast, 1995.
Armed loyalists of 3rd Battalion, North Belfast,
of Ulster Volunteer Force, with emblems of
Ulster Volunteer Force, Protestant Action Force and
Young Citizen Volunteers.
"Prepared for peace, ready for war."

Plate 99
Fountain area,
Derry, 1995.
King Billy crossing
the Boyne, and the
Siege of Derry, 1689.
Replica of
Bobby Jackson's mural,
originally painted
in the 1920s,
and repainted
each year until
wall fell down in 1994.

Plate 100
Sevastopol Street,
Belfast, 1995.
Bust of Bobby Sands,
and quotation from
his writings:
"Everyone, republican
or otherwise,
has his/her own
part to play".
Redesigned version of
original mural,
painted 1990.

THE FUTURE?

Plate 101
Short Strand,
Belfast, 1995.
Busts of local republicans
killed by loyalists, Éire,
Proclamation of the
Republic (1916), and
words of poem by
Bobby Sands.
"I measc laochra na
nGael go raibh a
nainmeacha"
(Their names are among
the heroes of the Gaels).

Plate 102
Flax Street,
Belfast, 1994.
Uileann piper on slopes
of Cave Hill.
Based on "The Blind
Piper"
by Joseph Hegarty.

54

Plate 103
Flax Street, Belfast, 1994.
Éire (or Ériu), mythological queen
slain in 1698 B.C.
"Meon an phobail a thógail tríd an chultúr"
(The people's spirit is raised through culture).

Plate 104
Flax Street,
Belfast, 1994.
Gaelic games - hurling,
camogie and football.
"Is treise dúchas ná
oiliuint"
(It is part of our
cultural heritage).

Plate 105
Falls Road,
Belfast, 1994.
Wards of West Belfast,
with total number of
unemployed.
Mural for European
week of action
against unemployment,
sponsored by
West Belfast Economic
Forum.

Plate 106
Falls Road, Belfast, 1995.
Mural commemorating 150th anniversary of
An Gorta Mór, the Great Famine.

Plate 107
Rosnareen Avenue, Belfast, 1995.
Mural commemorating 150th anniversary of the
Great Famine. "When the potato crop failed causing
'the Great Hunger' people watched in despair as
shiploads of food were escorted away by British troops..."

Plate 108
Beechmount Avenue,
Belfast, 1995.
Mural commemorating
150th anniversary of
the Great Famine.

Plate 109
Donegall Road,
Belfast, 1995.
Mural commemorating
150th anniversary of
the Great Famine.
Grosse Ile and
poem of Speranza.

Plate 110
New Lodge Road, Belfast, 1995.
Mural commemorating 150th anniversary of
the Great Famine.

THE FUTURE?

Plate 111
San Francisco, California,
photograph taken 1994.
Mural in solidarity with
struggle of
Palestinian people.

Plate 112
Mission District,
San Francisco,
California, 1994.
Mural on front of
Women's Building.